For You
and Me

For You and Me

Love Songs by
Paul Williams

 Hallmark Editions

from
Brand New Song

Somebody's singin' a brand new song.
There's somethin' in the words
you know you never heard before.
Somebody's singin' a brand new song.
It isn't a symphony,
just a simple melody,
but it's a song about love,
and we can always use one more.

I Won't
Last a Day
Without You

Day after day,
I must face a world of strangers
where I don't belong.
I'm not that strong.
It's nice to know
that there's someone
I can turn to
who will always care.
You're always there.

When there's no getting over that rainbow,
when my smallest of dreams won't come true,
I can take all the madness the world has to give,
but I won't last a day without you.

So many times,
when the city seems to be
without a friendly face,
a lonely place,
it's nice to know
that you'll be there
if I need you
and you'll always smile.
It's all worthwhile.

Touch me and I end up singing.
Troubles seem to up and disappear.
You touch me with the love you're bringing.
I can't really lose when you're near.

from
Let Me
Be the One

For love and understanding,
to find a quiet place,
for silent understanding,
a living touch,
come to me when things go wrong
and there's no love to light the way.
Let me be the one you run to.
Let me be the one you come to
when you need someone to turn to —
let me be the one.

All in All

Love is the warmth
that I've felt deep inside you,
sharing the silence of the dawn.
Love is the tenderness
of lying here beside you,
wondering where the night has gone.
All in all, I've had a taste
of the good and the bad.
Times spent in love
were the best that I've had.

Love is the taste
of your tears on my pillow.
Happiness always makes you cry.
And when your tiny back
is bending like a willow,
my dreams are chased across the sky.
All in all, we've had a taste
of the good and the bad.
Times spent in love
were the best that we've had.

You are the song
that the world should be singing.
Voices could rise and fill the air.
You are the happiness
we all might end up bringing
if we could only learn to share.
All in all, we've had a taste
of the good and the bad.
Times spent in love
were the best that we've had.

Let's Ride

Let's ride aboard a windy day.
We can hide behind the clouds
and disappear.
Sunshine can be so near.
It's a crime to throw your time away
when the world is ours
and there's so much to see.

Would you like to run away
where the grass is tall
and summer's in the air?
Just let me take you there.
We can try to find a hideaway
where the rain is warm
and happiness is free.

Rainy Days
and Mondays

Talkin' to myself and feelin' old.
Sometimes I'd like to quit.
Nothin' ever seems to fit.
Hangin' around,
nothin' to do but frown.
Rainy days and Mondays
always get me down.

What I've got, they used to call the blues.
Nothin' is really wrong.
Feelin' like I don't belong.
Walkin' around,
some kind of lonely clown.
Rainy days and Mondays
always get me down.

Funny but it seems
I always wind up here with you.
Nice to know somebody loves me.
Funny but it seems
that it's the only thing to do —
run and find the one who loves me.

What I feel has come and gone before.
No need to talk it out.
We know what it's all about.
Hangin' around,
nothin' to do but frown.
Rainy days and Mondays
always get me down.

from Trust

In a world of hidden treasure,
I have found the rainbow,
found it in you ....

from
Born to Fly

Is it wrong to say
"I love you" right away
to somebody new,
even though you know you do?
You decide what's right for you
and I'll decide for me.
You know where you're comin' from
and where you'd like to be.
All of us are different
as the snowflakes from the sky.
Snow was born to fall.
We were born to fly.

My Love and I

My love and I, learning from each other,
gathering roses on a rainy, do-nothin' day.
And in our room, lying in darkness,
we'll feel the sunshine on a cloudy day.
We can rise above the darkness
once love has swept the clouds away.

My love and I, turning to each other,
touching in silence while we talk of love with our eyes.
And in our room, no one can find us.
Resting together when the day is done,
we leave a troubled world behind us
and smile to think that we are one.
And if we change, we'll change together,
pick up the pieces if our dreams should fall,
put them back again together.
We've found the love to mend them all.

My love and I listen to each other,
live ev'ry moment
while the world outside rushes by.
And in our room, painted with laughter,
we've put our story in a song I play.
And we live happy ever after.
Our song will always end that way.

from
When Love
Is Far Away

Wishing helps to pass away
a rainy day,
a rainy afternoon
when love is far away.

Say Hello

Let's take some time
and get to know one another.
We'll solve our problems
if we do.
We may be different,
but we won't know till we try.
You can learn from me,
and I'll learn from you.

Love and understanding
opens up your eyes.
It clears the skies.
Let it show.
No, we don't need
to stay these worlds apart.
For a simple start—
say "hello."

Love for Everyone

Love, rising like the sun.
Love…
Love for everyone.
Love, a sunshine circus and calliope,
love, rising from a wishing well,
spinning like a carousel
and now there is you.
Love, waiting in a smile,
love, waiting all the while.
Love…
And now the time of love
has come for me.

from California Roses

You found a friend
in the lonely night
when you took my hand
and it felt just right.
Well, I knew even then
you were just what
I been lookin' for.
Oh, if you could learn
to depend on me,
I would show you the strength
of a great oak tree.
I'll be more than a friend
and you won't be alone
anymore.

I Never Had It So Good

I never had much money,
I never won a race,
my jokes don't end up funny,
and I've had doors
slammed in my face.
But I think you've charmed me.
I always hoped
that someone would.
I never had
a love like this before,
I never had it so good.

I'm not the type that's trusted,
always tripping over logs,
and often I've been busted,
and chased by friendly dogs.
But I think you've charmed me.
I always hoped
that someone would.
I never had
a love like this before,
I never had it so good.

from
I Know You

I know you. I know your face.
I've walked alone in the sun,
walks that would end in a run,
runs at a maddening pace
that would end in your arms,
my love, my love.

I'll never leave
'cause I need you for me,
need you to hold me this way,
need you to want me to stay.
I know you. I know your love.

In the Beginning

In the beginning,
empty pages
with our story still untold.
Yeah, love could find us
or pass behind us
or even blind us.
I don't know
and I don't pretend to know.

In the beginning,
only children
taking time to learn our song.
We'll sing together,
perhaps forever
or maybe never.
I don't know
and I don't pretend to know.

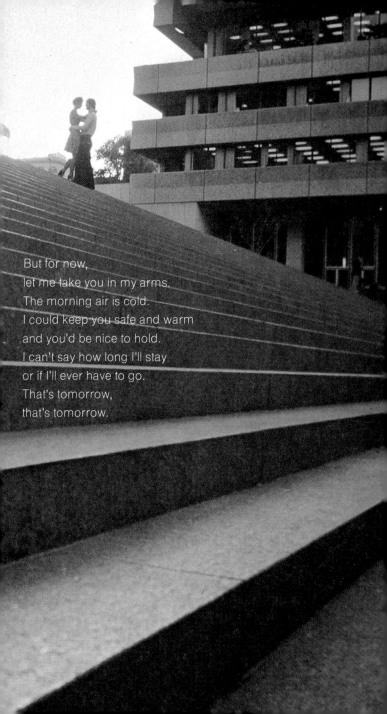

But for now,
let me take you in my arms.
The morning air is cold.
I could keep you safe and warm
and you'd be nice to hold.
I can't say how long I'll stay
or if I'll ever have to go.
That's tomorrow,
that's tomorrow.

Quiet Man

He's a quiet man.
Right or wrong, he never comes on strong.
He doesn't think that way.
He's a quiet man,
never shouts and if he doubts himself,
I really couldn't say.
But he has a way with me
sometimes hard to define.
Just what he feels for me,
I don't know.
He never lets it show,
but I love him so.

Catch that look in his eye
and you'll see for yourself
he's a hell of a man.
He's not likely to cry.
And I wonder sometimes
if he knows that he can.
I could be wrong —
I'd like to think he needs me.
I'm going to take that chance
and follow where he leads me.

from Does She Ever Think of Me

I think of the mornings,
little girl mornings,
    looking like innocence,
    sitting and sipping her first cup of tea.
And I remember her smiling.
Love kept her smiling.
And how I felt
sitting and watching
    and knowing her smile was for me.

from Lock, Stock and Barrel

Stormy weather, we've seen the last of you.
Good-day, sunshine!
Here's looking up to you.
You can have our love for good —
lock, stock and barrel.

The Lady.
Is Waiting

Brighter than neon
reflected on water,
the smile of the lady
is gracious and warm.
Though she's a woman,
she laughs like a child at play.
And the lady is waiting
at the end of my day.

Waits at the doorway
and says that she loves me
and wants me to tell her
that I love her, too.
If I have troubles,
I know she will wish them away.
And the lady is waiting
at the end of my day.

Waiting to comfort me
if I am weary. . . :
waiting to comfort me,
ready to cheer me,
ever so gentle
and kind.

And sharing my secrets
and wishing my wishes,
a whisper of summer
is there in her smile,
softly reflecting our love
in the things that we say.
And the lady is waiting
at the end of my day.

We've Only Just Begun

We've only just begun to live.
White lace and promises,
a kiss for luck and we're on our way.

Before the rising sun, we fly.
So many roads to choose.
We start out walking and learn to run.
And, yes, we've just begun.

Sharing horizons that are new to us,
watching the signs along the way,
talking it over, just the two of us,
working together day to day.
Together...

And when the evening comes, we smile,
so much of life ahead.
We'll find a place where there's room to grow.
And, yes, we've just begun to live.

When I
Was All Alone

People looked right through me
when I was all alone.
Never seemed to notice I was there at all,
always seemed to look the other way.
Winter days were colder when I was all alone.
Wasn't I surprised to feel this warm inside...
the way it feels to be alone with you.

So if I try to hold you,
and I might try
to make you stay,
remember I have tried
to hold the colors
of the morning sun,
tried to keep it shining
when the summer day
was done.

So you must know that I was lonely
when I was all alone.
Love was not an easy word to laugh about,
and still it's not an easy word to say.
When I was all alone,
wasn't I surprised to feel this warm inside...
the way it feels to be alone with you.

from
I Fell

To fall in love again
is to ride aboard
a windy carousel....

An Old Fashioned Love Song

Just an old fashioned love song,
coming down in three-part harmony.
Just an old fashioned love song,
one I'm sure they wrote for you and me
to weave our dreams upon
and listen to each evening
when the lights are low,
to underscore our love affair
with tenderness and feelings
that we've come to know.
You'll swear you've heard it before
as it slowly rambles on and on.
No need in bringing 'em back
'cause they've never really gone.
Just an old fashioned love song…
one I'm sure they wrote for you and me.

He's Comin' Home

It seems like only yesterday
that he set out to make it.
He gathered up his boyhood dreams
and showed them he could take it.
He's made his mark upon an unsuspecting world,
and now he's coming home.
This time he's coming home
to get his baby,
for his baby.

I knew that when he went away,
I'd have to live without him.
He swore that he'd be coming back.
I swore I'd think about him.
And now those lonely days are almost at an end.
Now, he's coming home.
This time he's coming home
to get his baby,
for his baby.

I'm still waiting.
Never once forgotten what his lovin'
meant to me.
He's had to learn a thing or two
while living in the city.
I wonder if he'll think I've changed
or if I'm still as pretty.
And now it won't be long until he's here with me.
He's coming home.
This time he's coming home
to get his baby,
for his baby.

Look What
I Found

Well, I walked all around
this crowded planet,
    but I walked all alone.
Though the places changed,
    the faces stayed the same.
Spendin' my money,
makin' up funny stories
    like you tell in a noisy bar
    where no one knows your name,
runnin' out of places
    still worth runnin' to,
takin' pictures
    no one's home to see,
makin' deals with small-town tourists
    traveling alone,
"I'll take one of you in Rome,
    if you'll take one of me."
And just when I'm givin' up
lookin' for love —
    look what I found!
Oh, look what I found.

Display titles set in Cheltenham Roman.
Body copy set in Helvetica Light.
Printed on Hallmark Crown Royale Book paper.

Edited by Tina Hacker.
Designed by Leanne Mishler.